I0574958

JOSEPH SMITH

Praise to the Man

PHOTOGRAPHY *by* John Telford
WRITTEN *by* Susan Easton Black

MILLENNIAL PRESS

MILLENNIAL PRESS, 576 S. Commerce Road, Suite #3, Orem, Utah 84058. millennialpress.com

ISBN: #1-932597-26-3 Printed in Singapore

"We were convinced that God was about to bring to light something that we might stay our minds upon, something that we could get a more definite idea of than anything which had been taught us heretofore. And we rejoiced in it with exceeding great joy." —*Lucy Mack Smith*

Contents

"The ends of the
Earth shall inquire
after thy Name."

— DOCTRINE AND COVENENTS 122:1

"HIS WORKS WILL LIVE TO ENDLESS AGES, AND UNNUMBERED MILLIONS YET UNBORN WILL MENTION HIS NAME WITH HONOR, AS A NOBLE INSTRUMENT IN THE HANDS OF GOD." — *Parley P. Pratt*

PREFACE

THE LAST DISPENSATION

"My testimony of him is that he was a true Prophet of God, raised up in this last dispensation of the fulness of times, and that his sayings and teachings are true and faithful."

— THOMAS COTTAM[1]

A PHOTOGRAPHIC JOURNEY OF THE PLACES FAMILIAR TO JOSEPH SMITH JR. IS SIMILAR TO LOOKING THROUGH A WINDOW INTO THE LIFE OF AN EXTRAORDINARY MAN. FROM HIS FIRST YOUTHFUL UTTERANCES IN THE PALMYRA WOODS to his manly cry at Carthage, Joseph was the "choice seer" whom the Lord raised up to bring forth the word of God. Revelations, translations, covenants, and eternal truths were the continuum of his life's labor for he held "the keys of this Last Dispensation, and will for ever hold them, both in time and eternity."[2] We know that "the Lord Almighty sealed upon [his] head every Priesthood, every key, every power, every principle that belongs to the last dispensation of the fullness of times, and to the building up of the kingdom of God."[3]

PAGE 6: *West Grove in Nauvoo* PAGE 7: *David's Chamber in Nauvoo*

"I had actually seen a light, and in the midst of that light I saw two Personages, and they did in reality speak to me; and though I was hated and persecuted for saying that I had seen a vision, yet it was true." —*Joseph Smith*

Perhaps Brigham Young said it best, "It was decreed in the councils of eternity, long before the foundations of the earth were laid, that he [Joseph Smith] should be the man, in the last dispensation of this world, to bring forth the word of God to the people, and receive the fullness of the keys and power of the Priesthood of the Son of God." We declare that Joseph Smith was "foreordained in eternity to preside over this last dispensation."[4]

We are not alone in our stance. Thousands of Latter-day Saints in the nineteenth-century resonated to Joseph Smith's declarations of prophetic revelation. Although contemporaries labeled them as odd, if not ordinary folk, there was nothing ordinary about their willingness to follow Joseph from New York to Illinois. Their hand-written journal entries reveal an unusual saga of courage and unflinching faith at a time when religious intolerance went unchecked. Their courage to withstand cruel persecution and encroaching evil, and their faith to look to God when all around them seemed to mock their convictions is an unparalleled story of religious faith. As the world tossed with waves of uncertainty in the nineteenth century, their strength became a beacon to those searching for eternal truths and Joseph Smith Jr., the man that each hoped one day to meet.

"I always believed in him from my first seeing him until his death, that he was the leader of this dispensation and God Almighty's prophet." — *William C. Staines*

"WHEN THE LIGHT RESTED UPON ME I SAW TWO PERSONAGES, WHOSE BRIGHTNESS AND GLORY DEFY ALL DESCRIPTION."

—*Joseph Smith*

"You knew he was a true prophet of God because you could not be in his presence without feeling the influence and Spirit of God, which seemed to flow from him almost as heat does from a stove. You could not see it, but you felt it," penned William Henrie.[5] Joseph L. Robinson noted that "the Prophet's voice was like the thunders of heaven, yet his language was meek and his instructions edified much. There was a power and majesty that attend his words and preaching that we never beheld in any man before."[6]

We are grateful to Millennial Press for the opportunity to present through the lenses of a photographic journey, the life of the Prophet of the latter days. Assisting us in this work has been Linda Sullivan as graphic designer, Heather Seferovich as editor, and Christina Smith as research assistant. We acknowledged the valuable assistance and wealth of knowledge gleaned from Karl Ricks Anderson. We are particularly grateful to Lachlan Mackay and the Community of Christ for assistance and permission to publish the photographs on pages 8, 36, 46, 50, 52 (bottom), 53, 54, 55, 56, 63, 87, 96 (left), 97, 99, and 104.

Within the colorful pages of *Joseph Smith: Praise to the Man*, readers discover the greatness of the man. Learn of his dogged determination to remain true to his convictions—even when faced with unrelenting persecution—and witness his reverence for the Divine. As two who know that Joseph Smith was called of God to lead this, the last dispensation, we present this photographic essay as our grateful remembrance of him.

PAGE 8: *Interior Kirtland Temple* PAGE 9: *Sacred Grove*

Communed With Jehovah

CHAPTER ONE

COMMUNED WITH JEHOVAH

"It is my meditation all the day, and more than my meat and drink to know how I shall make the saints of God comprehend the visions that roll like an overflowing surge before my mind."

—JOSEPH SMITH[1]

FATHER SMITH SAW FEW POSSIBILITIES OF MAKING AN ABUNDANT LIVING IN THE PICTURESQUE COUNTRYSIDE OF SHARON, VERMONT. PAST ECONOMIC SHENANIGANS OF UNSCRUPULOUS MEN HAD LEFT HIM WITH FEW OPTIONS AND EVEN LESS HOPE BY 1805. Fortune did allude Father Smith, and his family members knew it—Mother Lucy Mack Smith and their children—Alvin, Sophronia, and Hyrum. Poverty is never embraced as a welcomed guest. Its accompanying ills may have given Mother Smith pause as she anticipated delivering yet another child into her world of frequent disappointment. In announcing the birth of her newborn, she merely penned, "In the meantime we had a son, whom we called Joseph after the name of his father."[2] Thus, without fanfare on the wintry day of December 23, 1805 in Sharon, Vermont, Joseph Smith Jr. entered mortality, his destiny to restore Christ's church on earth.

His earliest years provided only the typical frontier options—exploring his environs and dwelling in a homemade log cabin. For young Joseph, relentless poverty stalked his family. His father tried his best at cultivating a farm on rocky soil. After harvesting meager crops, he found a school that needed a teacher for the winter months and this helped to make ends meet. Some years making a living as a farmer and a school teacher worked well but others were not well at all. After a time and "in this way ... our circumstances gradually improved," wrote Mother Smith. By 1811 yesteryears woes had passed, but "this state of things did not long continue."[3]

The hopeful move to West Lebanon, New Hampshire, proved to be an intense crucible for the Smiths. Typhus fever, an illness that had caused six thousand deaths in the Connecticut Valley, descended on the fledgling community. Smith children easily succumbed to the illness. Young Joseph, the future Prophet of the Restoration, was not excluded. He endured his two week bout with fever only to

PAGES 10–11: *Sacred Grove* PAGE 12: *Joseph Smith Sr. Log Home*

"Sacred to the memory of Joseph Smith the Prophet, Born here, 23rd December, 1805. Martyred, Carthage, Illinois, 27th June 1844." — *Inscription on Monument*

discover that this was the beginning of a struggle that would mar his early years.

A local doctor's unwise lancing of an infection on Joseph's arm brought more pain than relief. "Oh, father! the pain is so severe," cried Joseph. "How can I bear it!"[4] Bear it he must for "the disease removed and ascended into my left leg and ankle and terminated in a fever sore of the worst kind," wrote Joseph. The advice of physicians at Dartmouth Medical College was sought to help the young boy. They suggested amputating the boy's foot as an option. Young Joseph protested: "Young as I was, I utterly refused to give my assent to the operation."[5]

A less obtrusive surgery was then presented as a second option. After consideration, Joseph agreed to this operation. Father Smith, learning of his son's consent, cast "his eyes upon his boy,... [and] burst into a flood of tears."[6] Although the procedure ultimately relieved pain and a diseased portion of the bone, "Joseph [became] pale as a corpse."[7] Afterward, "fourteen additional pieces of bone" worked their way out of the incision.[8] During these difficult days, Uncle Jesse Smith agreed to care for young Joseph in his home on the coast of Massachusetts until he recovered. Sea breezes and constant care helped Joseph's health stabilize. He then rejoined his family—a family who once again was facing poverty.

"We were compelled to strain every energy to provide for our present necessities, instead of making arrangements for the future," wrote Lucy. Hoping better land in the state of Vermont would provide needed economic relief, the Smiths sought rental property in rural Norwich. Father Smith tilled the soil but farming seemed not to be his lot in life, his every effort failed. "The first year our crops failed;... The crops the second year were as the year before—a perfect failure....

PAGE 14: *Joseph Smith Monument in Sharon, Vermont*
PAGE 15 LEFT: *Dartmouth Medical College* RIGHT: *Wheat field in Sharon, Vermont*

"At one time eleven Doctors came from Dartmouth Medical College, at Hanover, New Hampshire, for the purpose of amputation, but, young as I was, I utterly refused to give my assent to the operation." —*Joseph Smith*

The next year an untimely frost destroyed the crops." Discouraged by the crop failings, Lucy said, "This was enough."[9]

In 1816, Father Smith ventured from Vermont seeking a suitable locale in which to relocate his family. It wasn't until he reached Palmyra, New York, that his imagination was captured. Stately trees, the proposed Erie Canal, and cheap prices for "virgin farmland" held promises of a brighter future for him. He moved and began working as a hired hand. In the meanwhile, opportunist Caleb Howard was employed to transport Mother Smith and children to the western clime of Palmyra. En route to what would soon become young Joseph's land of destiny, Howard proved himself "an unprincipled and unfeeling wretch." He forced young Joseph "to travel miles at a time on foot, notwithstanding he was still lame."[10] Howard spent the money he held in trust for the Smiths "drinking & gambling." Joseph stated, "I suffered the most excruciating

"In this place we established ourselves on a farm belonging to one Esquire Murdock. The first year our crops failed.... The crops the second year were as the year before a perfect failure.... The next year an untimely frost destroyed the crops.... This was enough; my husband was now altogether decided upon going to New York." —*Lucy Mack Smith*

"IT WAS ON THE MORNING OF A BEAUTIFUL, CLEAR DAY, EARLY IN THE SPRING OF EIGHTEEN HUNDRED AND TWENTY." —*Joseph Smith*

weariness & pain [at his hands and was] ... left to wallow in my blood." But for the kindness of a stranger who "picked me up, & carried me to the Town" Joseph may not have reached Palmyra.[11]

In the fledgling community, he was united with his family—a family with only "a small portion of our affects, and barely two cents in cash." Once again, the Smiths had become "much reduced—not from indolence, but on account of many reverses of fortune, with which our lives had been rather singularly marked."[12] Hoping to put behind them what was becoming an alarming economic situation, all able bodied family members looked for ways to improve the family's finances. Father Smith opened a small bakeshop on Main street, offering customers gingerbread, pies, and root beer. Mother Smith used her artistic talents to paint oil-cloth coverings. Joseph's siblings found jobs as common labors rocking up wells and working as farmhands.

The Smiths' hard work began to pay off. By 1818 they had saved enough to contract for a hundred-acre farm. The contracted farm was in a beautiful setting in a wooded tract about two miles south of the Palmyra village. From the beginning the mortgaged farm venture proved successful. "I believe something like thirty acres of land were got ready for cultivation the first year," wrote Mother Smith. By the second year she boasted, "We had a snug loghouse, neatly furnished, and the means of living comfortably."[13] Within two years, the Smiths had turned their wooded acreage into a productive farm "admired for its good order and industry."[14]

And on the heels of their success came a sense of belonging, a sense of ownership, and a sense of permanence to the family. "If we might judge by external manifestations," wrote Mother Smith, "we had every reason to believe that we had many good and affectionate friends for never have

"I HAVE ACTUALLY SEEN A VISION; AND WHO AM I THAT I CAN WITHSTAND GOD, OR WHY DOES THE WORLD THINK TO MAKE ME DENY WHAT I HAVE ACTUALLY SEEN?" — *Joseph Smith*

I seen more kindness or attention shown to any person or family than we received from those around us."[15]

Surprisingly, in early spring of 1820 cordial neighbors turned from friend to foe. It wasn't any untoward action of Father or Mother Smith that caused the alienation. A curious message told to an itinerant minister by the fourteen-year-old Joseph Smith Jr. caused townsfolk to withdraw fellowship. Youthful Joseph told the preacher that he had seen a heavenly vision on his family farm. Oddly enough, the mere mention of this truth sparked a flame of Smith hatred that went unchecked in Palmyra for years. The teenager's unwavering affirmation that God the Father and his Son Jesus Christ appeared to him in the Palmyra woods did not help the damaged social situation for the Smiths.

Even though men in town boasted of heavenly raptures of their own, it was the grandiose account of Joseph's First Vision that rancored the community. Community leaders wanted only confessing, if sometimes contending Christians who professed salvation, justice, and grace to live in their town. They wanted a community of upstanding citizens who shouted praises to God. They didn't want living among them a young boy who claimed that he knew better than they. "Priest contending against priest, and convert against convert" was acceptable, not the challenging views of young Joseph.[16]

It is remarkable that under such severe pressure from so many, Joseph refused to veer from his conviction that he had seen "a pillar of light exactly over my head, above

PAGE 16 : *Joseph Smith Sr. Farm* PAGE 17: *Sacred Grove*

"WE NEVER KNEW WE WERE BAD FOLKS UNTIL JOSEPH TOLD HIS VISION. WE WERE CONSIDERED RESPECTABLE TILL THEN, BUT AT ONCE PEOPLE BEGAN TO CIRCULATE FALSEHOODS." — *William Smith*

the brightness of the sun, which descended gradually until it fell upon me.... When the light rested upon me I saw two Personages, whose brightness and glory defy all description, standing above me in the air. One of them spake unto me, calling me by name and said, pointing to the other—This is My Beloved Son. Hear Him!" Jesus Christ told Joseph that he must not unite himself with any denomination for "all their creeds were an abomination in his sight; that those professors were all corrupt." The divine answer to Joseph was clear but not to townsfolk who tried to convince him that his vision was, "all of the devil, that there were no such things as visions or revelations in these days; that all such things had ceased with the apostles."[17] Then, as if to censor the boy for his resolute stance, ministers and farmers withdrew from him and cast aspersions upon not only the teenager but the whole Smith family.

"Though I was an obscure boy, only between fourteen and fifteen years of age, and my circumstances in life such as to make a boy of no consequence in the world," Joseph recalled, "yet men of high standing would take notice sufficient to excite the public mind against me, and create a bitter persecution." In the wake of persecution came ostracism and personal sorrow to Joseph and his family. Yet nothing could make the boy deny that he had seen divine beings in the woods on his family farm. "I had actually seen a light, and in the midst of that light I saw two Personages, and they did in reality speak to me; and though I was hated and persecuted for saying that I had seen a vision, yet it was true;... I knew it, and I knew that God knew it, and I could not deny it."[18]

Epithets such as "lazy," "illiterate," "superstitious," "disorderly," "a drunkard," "an imposter," and "addicted to vice and the grossest immoralities" were words hurled at the youth.[19] When farmer Thomas Taylor was asked, "Why didn't they like [young Joseph]?" He answered, "To tell the truth, there was something about him they could not understand; some way he knew more than they did, and it made them mad."[20] Townsfolk became so mad that some refused to hire any Smith family member for even a menial chore. "We never knew we were bad folks until Joseph told his vision," penned Joseph's younger brother William. "We were considered respectable till then, but at once people began to circulate falsehoods and stories."[21]

One church-going man said, "The very influence the boy carried was the danger they feared for the coming generation, that not only the young men, but all

PAGE 18: *Interior of Joseph Smith Sr. Log Home (restored)*
PAGE 19: *Joseph Smith Sr. Framehouse in Palmyra (restored)*

"We were still making arrangements to build us a comfortable house, the management and control of which evolved chiefly upon Alvin." —*Lucy Mack Smith*

"While I was thus in the act of calling upon God, I discovered a light appearing in my room, which continued to increase until the room was lighter than at noonday, when immediately a personage appeared at my bedside, standing in the air, for his feet did not touch the floor." —*Joseph Smith History 1:30*

"HE SAID THERE WAS A BOOK DEPOSITED, WRITTEN UPON GOLD PLATES, GIVING AN ACCOUNT OF THE FORMER INHABITANTS OF THIS CONTINENT, AND THE SOURCE FROM WHENCE THEY SPRANG."

—*Joseph Smith History 1:34*

who came in contact with him, would follow him and he must be put down."[22] The mob-like tone of his sentiment was followed by a bullet intended for young Joseph. These lawless actions caused Joseph great sorrow but were minor in comparison to thoughts about his own behavior—a behavior in which he "frequently fell into many foolish errors, and displayed the weakness of youth, and the foibles of human nature."[23] He confessed, "I have not, neither can it be sustained, in truth, been guilty of wronging or injuring any man or society of men."[24] For one who had talked with Heavenly Beings face to face and had suffered "severe persecution at the hands of all classes of men, both religious and irreligious, because I continued to affirm that I had seen a vision," his behavior caused self-condemnation.[25]

On the evening of September 21, 1823, Joseph pled "for forgiveness of all my sins and follies, and also for a manifestation to me, that I might know of my state and standing before him." While praying, "I discovered a light appearing in my room, which continued to increase until the room was lighter than at noonday, when immediately a personage appeared at my bedside, standing in the air, for his feet did not touch the floor." The angelic personage "called me by name, and said unto me that he was a messenger sent from the presence of God to me, and that his name was Moroni."[26]

From Moroni, Joseph learned that "God had a work for me to do; and that my name should be had for good and evil among all nations, kindreds, and tongues, or that it should be both good and evil ... spoken of

PAGE 20: *Interior of Joseph Smith Sr. Log Home (second floor)*
PAGE 21: *Monuments of the Angel Moroni*

"We all with one accord wept over our irretrievable loss, and we could 'not be comforted, because [Alvin] was not.'" —*Lucy Mack Smith*

"The sweetest union and happiness pervaded our house. No jar nor discord disturbed our peace, and tranquility reigned in our midst." —*Lucy Mack Smith*

"[The Book of Mormon record] was hid in the earth by Moroni, in a hill called by him, Cumorah, which hill is now in the State of New York, near the village of Palmyra." — Oliver Cowdery

among all people." He was then told of a book written upon plates that had the appearance of gold and of a Urim and Thummim that had been prepared to help him translate these plates. As the angel spoke of these sacred things, "the place [the hill] where the plates were deposited" was shown him in vision. When the illuminating scene ended, the angel departed. Before dawn, however, the angelic messenger reappeared again and again until his visits "occupied the whole of that night."[27]

The next morning, Joseph arose from his bed with plans to go about the "necessary labors of the day" in the fields. He went to the fields but in so doing discovered that his strength was gone. He then began to walk toward the family home. As he did so his steps were arrested when the angel again appeared and "related unto me all that he had related to me the previous night, and commanded me to go to my father and tell him of the vision and commandments which I had received." In compliance, Joseph retraced his steps to the field and told his father of the angel and his message. "It was of God," affirmed Father Smith.[28]

Joseph went to the place shown him in vision—"a hill of considerable size, and the most elevated of any in the neighborhood." There on the hill, he discovered "under a stone of considerable size, lay the plates, deposited in a stone box." He attempted to remove the plates from its receptacle, but was prevented by the same heavenly messenger. "The time for bringing them forth had not yet arrived," Joseph was told and would not "until he had learned to keep the commandments of God—not only till he was willing but able to do it."[29]

Four years passed before twenty-one-year-old Joseph was given the plates and the Urim and Thummim. During that interim, "he would describe the ancient inhabitants of this continent, their dress, mode of travelling, and the animals upon which they rode; their cities, their buildings, with every particular; their mode of warfare; and also their religious worship. This he would do with as much ease,

PAGE 22: *Tombstone of Alvin Smith at the John Swift Memorial Cemetery in Palmyra* PAGES 22–23: *Interior of Joseph Smith Sr. Framehouse (restored)* PAGE 24: *Statue of Angel Moroni on the Hill Cumorah* PAGE 25: *Kitchen at the Joseph Smith Sr. Framehouse (restored)* PAGE 25: *Cornerstone to Joseph Smith Jr. Home in Harmony, Pennsylvania*

"[JOSEPH] DETERMINED THAT A PORTION OF THE HEARTH SHOULD BE TAKEN UP, AND THE RECORD AND BREAST-PLATE SHOULD BE BURIED UNDER THE SAME, AND THEN THE HEARTH BE RE-LAID, TO PREVENT SUSPICION." —*Lucy Mack Smith*

"THE BUSINESS IN WHICH MY FATHER WAS ENGAGED OFTEN REQUIRED HIM TO HAVE HIRED HELP, AND AMONG THE MANY HE FROM TIME TO TIME EMPLOYED WAS A YOUNG MAN BY THE NAME OF JOSEPH SMITH, JUN., TO WHOM I WAS PARTICULARLY ATTACHED. HIS NOBLE DEPORTMENT, HIS FAITHFULNESS, AND HIS KIND ADDRESS COULD NOT FAIL TO WIN THE ESTEEM OF THOSE WHO HAD THE PLEASURE OF HIS ACQUAINTANCE." — *Newel Knight*

seemingly, as if he had spent his whole life among them," recalled his mother.[30] His brother William was asked, "Did you not doubt Joseph's testimony sometimes?" He replied, "No we all had implicit confidence in what he said. He was a truthful boy. Father and Mother believed him; why should not the children?"[31] The Smith family was "confirmed in the opinion that God was about to bring to light something upon which we could stay our minds, or that would give us a more perfect knowledge of the plan of salvation and the redemption of the human family." Their conviction of forthcoming truth led Mother Smith to pen, "Tranquility reigned in our midst."[32]

Unfortunately, there was more than tranquility reigning for the Smiths in Palmyra. A mob element in

"Upon you my fellow servants, in the name of Messiah, I confer the Priesthood of Aaron, which holds the keys of the ministering of angels, and of the gospel of repentance, and of baptism by immersion for the remission of sins." — *Doctrine and Covenants 13*

the community was threatening physical violence. The death of Alvin Smith and the marriage of Joseph to Emma Hale of Harmony, Pennsylvania, did not temper the lawless. When Joseph received the gold plates on September 27, 1827 "with this charge: that I should be responsible for them; that if I should let them go carelessly, or through any neglect of mine, I should be cut off," it was not an idle warning.[33] "Satan had now stirred up the hearts of those who had gotten a hint of the matter," wrote Joseph, "to search into it and make every possible move towards thwarting the purposes of the Almighty." Mobs shouted, "We will have them plates in spite of Joe Smith or all the devils in hell."[34] Knowing their determination, Joseph hid the plates in sundry places around the family farm hoping to keep thieves at bay.

Instead of being frustrated by his tactics, the would-be thieves grew more vigilant in their efforts. To keep the plates safe, Joseph and his wife, Emma, found it best to leave Palmyra. For a time, they lived at the home of Emma's father, Isaac Hale, in Harmony, Pennsylvania. The Hale home provided a brief respite until Father Hale discovered Joseph had secret contents that he could not see. Joseph and Emma then sought a home of their own in Harmony. In their own abode, a son was born who died just a few hours after his birth and the Book of Lehi was translated, only to have the manuscript of the book that Martin Harris took misplaced, if not stolen.

After these tragedies, there came a sense of peace into their home—a blessing associated with translating and scribing the Book of Mormon. Emma recalled, "I am satisfied that no man could have dictated the writing of the manuscripts unless he was inspired." Explaining the process, Emma continued, "When acting as his scribe, [he] would dictate to me hour after hour; and when returning after meals, or after interruptions, he would at once begin where he had left off, without either seeing the manuscript or having any portion of it read to him." As Emma affirmed, "This was a usual thing for him to do. It would have been improbable that a learned man could do this; and, for one so ignorant and unlearned as he was, it was simply impossible."[35] Scribe Oliver Cowdery added, "These were days never to

PAGE 26: *Monument Commemorating the Aaronic Priesthood in Harmony*
PAGE 27 LEFT: *Susquehanna River* RIGHT: *Tombstone of Son of Joseph and Emma Smith in Harmony*

"While the veil was parted and the angel of God came down clothed in glory, and delivered the anxiously looked for message, and the keys of the gospel of repentance! What joy! what wonder! what amazement!...our eyes behold—our ears heard." — *Oliver Cowdery*

be forgotten—to sit under the sound of a voice dictated by the inspiration of heaven, awakened the utmost gratitude of this bosom.... to write from his mouth, as he translated, with the Urim and Thummim ... the history, or record, called 'The book of Mormon.'"[36]

On May 15, 1829, Joseph and Oliver "went into the woods to pray and inquire of the Lord respecting baptism for the remission of sins, that we found mentioned in the translation of the plates." While they prayed near the Susquehanna River, a messenger sent from heaven, known in the New Testament as John the Baptist, "descended in a cloud of light, and having his hands upon us, ordained" Joseph and Oliver to the Aaronic Priesthood. He then commanded that they "go and be baptized," which they did.[37] After his baptism, Joseph "prophesied concerning the rise of this church, and many other things connected with the Church, and this generation of the children of men."[38]

"In memory of
An Infant Son of
Joseph and Emma Smith
June 15th 1828."
— *epitaph*

"THE TABLE WAS SET BEFORE US AND ON IT THE RECORDS WERE PLACED. THE RECORDS OF THE NEPHITES, FROM WHICH THE BOOK OF MORMON WAS TRANSLATED, THE BREAST PLATES, THE BALL OF DIRECTORS, THE SWORD OF LABAN AND OTHER PLATES. WHILE WE WERE VIEWING THEM THE VOICE OF GOD SPOKE OUT OF HEAVEN SAYING THAT THE BOOK WAS TRUE AND THE TRANSLATION CORRECT." — *David Whitmer*

Next came the restoration of the Melchizedek Priesthood by the ancient apostles—Peter, James, and John. "I was also present with Joseph," wrote Oliver, "when the higher or Melchizedek Priesthood was conferred by holy angels from on high."[39] With his priesthood came the blessings of greater light and knowledge. "Our minds being now enlightened," wrote Joseph, "we began to have the scriptures laid open to our understandings, and the true meaning and intention of their more mysterious passages revealed unto us."[40]

The days of basking in the word of the Lord ended all too soon for Joseph and Oliver. Persecution with all its ills reared in Harmony and forced them to put aside the sacred and solve the pressing issue of safety. In May 1829 Joseph and Oliver fled from mobocracy in Harmony to the farmhouse of Peter Whitmer Sr. in Fayette, New York. Once safely sequestered in the Whitmer home, the translation resumed. As completion of the translation neared, three witnesses—Oliver Cowdery, David Whitmer, and Martin Harris—were shown the ancient engraved plates by the angelic messenger. The witnesses' stirring testimonies of what they had seen and heard moved Joseph to say, "I am not any longer to be entirely alone in the world."[41]

The testimony of these three men was written in the front pages of the published Book of Mormon. Their testimony and the publication of the book itself caused friends, near neighbors, and even strangers to take sides for or against the book. Those convinced of the truth of the Book of Mormon, like Joseph's sister Katherine Smith, knew that "without God's guidance [my] brother could not have brought forth such a work ... Many times when I have read its sacred pages, I have wept like a child, while the Spirit has borne witness with my spirit of its truth."[42] Believers, like Katherine, looked

PAGE 28: *Three Witnesses Monument in Richmond, Missouri*
PAGE 29: *House on Martin Harris Farm in Palmyra*

"I command thee that thou shalt not covet thine own property, but impart it freely to the printing of the Book of Mormon, which contains the truth and the word of God." — *Doctrine and Covenants 19:26*

"The size of the page was agreed upon, and an estimate ... that a page of manuscript would make more than a page of printed matter, which proved to be correct. The contract was to print and bind with leather, 5000 copies for $3,000."

–*John H. Gilbert,* Typesetter

"EVERY CHAPTER, IF I REMEMBER CORRECTLY, WAS ONE SOLID PARAGRAPH, WITHOUT A PUNCTUATION MARK, FROM BEGINNING TO END. NAMES OF PERSONS AND PLACES WERE GENERALLY CAPITALIZED, BUT SENTENCES HAD NO END ... I PUNCTUATED IT TO MAKE IT READ AS I SUPPOSED THE AUTHOR INTENDED." —*John H. Gilbert,* Typesetter

forward to the fulfillment of the Lord's promise, "If this generation harden not their hearts, I will establish my church among them."[43]

About fifty such believers met on Tuesday, April 6, 1830, in the log home of Peter Whitmer Sr. for the first meeting of what would become The Church of Jesus Christ of Latter-day Saints. The meeting began with prayer. After the sacrament of the Lord's Supper was blessed and passed to those assembled, "the Holy Ghost was poured out upon us to a very great degree—some prophesied, whilst we all praised the Lord, and rejoiced exceedingly."[44] Twenty-five-year-old Joseph Smith was then recognized by the assemblage as "a seer, a translator, a prophet, an apostle of Jesus Christ, an elder of the church through the will of God the Father, and the grace of your Lord Jesus Christ."[45]

At the close of the meeting, Father and Mother Smith stepped forward and requested baptism. At the water's edge, Joseph exclaimed, "Praise to my God! that I lived to see my own father baptized into the true Church of Jesus Christ!"[46] Joseph witnessed other baptisms that day and in the days to come, for the Church established in Fayette was "like a grain of mustard seed, which a man took, and sowed in his field: ... when it is grown, it is the greatest among herbs."[47] The newly baptized declared the truth of the Book of Mormon and accepted mission calls to spread the gospel of Jesus Christ and bring souls unto Him.

PAGES 30–31: *Exterior and Interior of E. B. Grandin Bookstore (restored) and Book of Mormon Press*

"That house will, no doubt, be celebrated for ages to come as the one chosen by the Lord in which to make known the first elements of the organization of His Kingdom in the latter days." — *Orson Pratt*

"THESE WERE DAYS NEVER TO BE FORGOTTEN—TO SIT UNDER THE SOUND OF A VOICE DICTATED BY THE INSPIRATION OF HEAVEN, AWAKENED THE UTMOST GRATITUDE OF THIS BOSOM." — *Oliver Cowdery*

"Many opened their houses to us," penned Joseph. "Our meetings were well attended, and many began to pray fervently to Almighty God, that He would give them wisdom to understand the truth."[48] The young and the old, the learned and the illiterate listened and embraced the teachings of the new church. Among their number was Warren Foote. "[I] frequently prayed to the Lord in secret to guide me in the right way," he wrote.[49] After carefully comparing the teachings of the Book of Mormon with those of the Bible, Foote joined the Church. Thus, the gospel spread from person to person, and from village to village, in New York before moving onto Ohio.

PAGE 32: *Peter Whitmer Sr. Log Home in Fayette, New York (restored)*
PAGE 33 LEFT: *Interior of Whitmer Log Home where Church was organized on April 6, 1830* RIGHT: *Translation Room in the Whitmer Home*
BOTTOM: *Baptismal site at Seneca Lake.*

Keys He Will Hold

M.P.C. M.P.C. M.P.C.
P.M.H. P.M.H. P.M.H.
M.H.P. M.H.P. M.H.P.
P. E. P. E.
M. M.

CHAPTER TWO

KEYS HE WILL HOLD

"You knew he was a true prophet of God because you could not be in his presence without feeling the influence and Spirit of God, which seemed to flow from him almost as heat does from a stove. You could not see it, but you felt it."

—William Henrie[1]

"The people thronged us night and day, insomuch that we had no time for rest or retirement," wrote missionary Parley P. Pratt of his stint near Kirtland, Ohio.[2] Most notable of the throng was a preacher named Sidney Rigdon. Rigdon advised those who listened to the missionary, "Prove all things and hold fast that which is good."[3] Over a hundred held fast, entered baptismal waters and emerged as Latter-day Saints. Like the Saints of biblical times, those in the last dispensation of time would also witness joy and sorrow, peace and upheaval, loyalty and betrayal.

Most unusual about these first converts in Ohio was their refusal to discard the "gifts of the spirit" of their old-time religion. At Latter-day Saint meetings the newly baptized clamored for a chance to show off their "god-given" abilities—questionable revelations and unusual physical movements. Some would "swoon away, and make unseemly gestures, and be drawn or disfigured in their countenances. Others would fall into ecstacies, and be drawn into contortions, cramps, fits, etc. Others would seem to have visions and revelations, which were not edifying, and which were not congenial to the doctrine and spirit of the gospel. In short, a false and lying spirit seemed to be creeping into the Church."[4] Failure to discern between the "strange notions and false spirits" led to differences of opinion and wide-spread doctrinal confusion within the Latter-day Saint congregation.[5] So widespread did the confusion become that converts expressed aloud their belief that only the Prophet Joseph himself could set the Church in order. It appears the Lord Jesus Christ agreed for in December 1830, Joseph and his New York followers were commanded to "assemble together at the Ohio."[6]

PAGES 34–35: *Fairport Harbor* PAGE 36: *Interior of Kirtland Temple*

"In Kirtland, when wagon loads of grown people and children came in from the country to meeting, Joseph would make his way to as many of the wagons as he well could and cordially shake the hand of each person." —*Louisa Littlefield*

With some reluctance the Smiths, Whitmers, Knights, and others left hearth and home to obey the divine directive. Peter Whitmer sold his Fayette acreage and farmhouse for $2,200 before leaving. Others also sold properties, but not at such a favorable return. "As might be expected, we were obliged to make great sacrifices of our property," penned Newel Knight.[7] A few believed Phoebe Carter sacrificed more. "When the time came for my departure I dared not trust myself to say farewell; so I wrote my good-byes to each, and leaving them on my table, ran downstairs and jumped into the carriage. Thus I left the beloved home of my childhood to link my life with the saints of God," she wrote.[8]

Joining the exodus of Phoebe and other New York co-religionists was the Prophet Joseph and his wife, Emma. They arrived on February 1, 1831, at the N. K. Whitney and Co. store in Kirtland. "You've prayed me here, now what do you want of me?" Joseph asked storekeeper Newel K. Whitney.[9] The answer: set in order the Church. The Prophet was needed to teach the Ohio Saints about discerning the Spirit, the workings of the priesthood, and keeping the commandments of God.

PAGES 38–39: *Exterior and interior of Newel K. Whitney and Co. Store in Kirtland*

"Newel K. Whitney! Thou art the man!" said Joseph. "You have the advantage of me, I could not call you by name, as you have me," replied Newel. "I am Joseph, the Prophet. You've prayed me here; now what do you want of me?" — *Orson F. Whitney*

Over the next several years he would do just that, but for now there were new friends, like Mary Elizabeth Rollins, to greet. "I have never saw anything like it on the earth," she wrote. "I could not take my eyes off him."[10] Convert Brigham Young was more impressed with the Prophet's doctrinal teachings than his personage: "What a delight it was to hear brother Joseph talk upon the great principles of eternity; he would bring them down to the capacity of a child, and he would unite heaven with earth."[11]

Not all were pleased that Joseph and his followers were gathering to Ohio. The editor of the *Painesville Telegraph* expressed discomfort at seeing "about two hundred men, women and children, of the deluded followers of Jo Smith's Bible speculation, have arrived on our coast ... from New York." He feared, "If the growth of the Church were not soon halted, inhabitants of Kirtland would be governed by the revelations of the Mormon Prophet."[12] In hindsight that may not have been so bad, though non-Mormon neighbors might not have agreed. To them Mormonism was a growing menace and stopping it short of bloodshed seemed increasingly impossible.

As the numbers of Latter-day Saints continued to swell, Ohioans noted with some concern that Mormonism attracted the destitute to their doorsteps. "If any man that ever did gather with the Saints was any poorer than I was—it was because he had nothing," said Brigham Young. "I had two children to take care of—that was all. I was a widower," he said. Joseph asked, "Brother Brigham, had you any shoes?" Brigham replied, "No, not a shoe to my foot, except a pair of borrowed boots."[13] Whatever their economic circumstances, neither poverty nor discomfort stopped the flow of Mormon faithful to Ohio. So great were their numbers, one journalist announced the "whole world" would soon be living in rural Kirtland. His prediction was absurd. However, available housing in the area soon filled and boxes were appropriated for shelter until permanent arrangements could be secured for all.

Latter-day Saints who gathered to Ohio sought occasions to be near Joseph Smith, the man they viewed as a Prophet of God. They were so taken by his divine appointment that any untoward statement, "false reports, lies, and foolish stories" casting slurs or aspersions on his character were immediately countered.[14] None were more vigilant in the Prophet's defense than Brigham Young. When he heard a man yelling, "Woe! woe! unto the inhabitants of this place, I put my pants and shoes

"I next went into the store of Gilbert and Whitney in Kirtland to serve as clerk, where I continued for a year or two." — *Orson Hyde*

"When I came out of the water, I knew that I had been born of water and of the spirit, for my mind was illuminated with the Holy Ghost.... The next morning I started home a happy man." —*Philo Dibble*

on, took my cow-hide, went out, and laying hold on him, jerked him round, and assured him that if he did not stop his noise and let the people enjoy their sleep without interruption, I would cow-hide him on the spot, for we had the Lord's Prophet right here, and we did not want the Devil's prophet yelling round the streets."[15]

Knowing of the fierce loyalty of his followers, some might deduce that Joseph was shielded from any and all verbal and physical abuse and that the overt persecution he had known in New York was non-existent in Ohio. Such a deduction would be false. Try as they may, not even Brigham Young could protect Joseph from the ordeal of March 24, 1832 that began at the John Johnson farmhouse in Hiram, Ohio. That evening, he and Emma took turns caring for their eleven-month-old twins, ill from the effects of measles. As the night hours waned, Joseph slept while Emma comforted her little ones until a dozen men with blackened faces broke into their bedroom. The intruders grabbed at Joseph's "shirt, drawers and limbs." His struggle to free himself spawned threats of death from the lawless men in his room. "[This] quieted me," Joseph said.[16]

PAGE 40: *Interior of Newel K. Whitney and Co. Store* PAGE 41: *Chagrin Falls*

"We repaired to the water, (the Chagrin River which flows through Kirtland) and, after a season of prayer, Brother Joseph Smith, Jr., baptized us by immersion." — *Ebenezer Robinson*

"You will have mercy and spare my life, I hope," he pled. The profane response was, "Call on yer God for help, we'll show ye no mercy." They then proceeded to "beat and scratch me well, tear off my shirt and drawers, and leave me naked," Joseph said.[17] Tar and feathers followed—feathers to symbolize that these men openly mocked Joseph and his teachings. Confident that their dark deed had left their victim dead, they scattered into the shadows of the night.

Joseph did not die that night as the mob had planned. He was merely unconscious when the mobbers fled. When consciousness returned, he tried to stand upon his feet but could not. By exerting himself a second time, he arose. He then cautiously moved toward the farmhouse from which he had been dragged. Once inside the house, distraught followers carefully removed the tar from his "scarified and defaced" body.[18]

The shameful hand of oppression had worked its craft well that night—a prophet of God had reeled in pain. What would his reaction be to the mobocratic rule? Rather than curse God for his woes, Joseph spoke of comfort. "God is my friend—in him I shall find comfort. I have given my life into his hands.... I Count not my life dear to me only to do his will."[19]

PAGE 42: *East Fork of the Chagrin River* PAGE 43: *Isaac Morley Farm in Kirtland*

"The Prophet called on all who held the Priesthood to gather into the little log school house they had [on the Morley Farm]. It was a small house, perhaps fourteen feet square. But it held the whole of the Priesthood of the Church of Jesus Christ of Latter-day Saints who were then in the town of Kirtland." — *Wilford Woodruff*

"On the 12th of September, I removed with my family to the township of Hiram, and commenced living with John Johnson." —*Joseph Smith*

"[Myself and Emma] received every kindness and attention which could be expected, and especially from Sister Whitney." —*Joseph Smith*

In speaking of his loyal followers, he said, "Our trust is in God, and we are determined, His grace assisting us, to maintain the cause and hold out faithful unto the end."[20] His well-chosen words encouraged Mormons to turn their thoughts from vengeance, and return to their sickles and plows and bring order from lawlessness and beauty to Kirtland.

To outsiders, the Latter-day Saints overcame opposition and built as if Kirtland would be their permanent home. With renewed strength their construction continued at a pace, heretofore, unknown. Businesses and mercantile establishments sprang up seemingly overnight. Under the name of the Church a printing office and bank plus sundry work places—a general store, blacksmith

PAGE 44 LEFT: *John Johnson Home in Hiram* RIGHT: *Newel K. Whitney Home in Kirtland* PAGE 45: *Interior of the John Johnson Home*

"I resumed the translation of the Scriptures. From sundry revelations which had been received, it was apparent that many important points touching the salvation of men, had been taken from the Bible, or lost before it was compiled." —*Joseph Smith*

"I SAW HIS COUNTENANCE LIGHTED UP AS THE INSPIRATION OF THE HOLY GHOST RESTED UPON HIM, DICTATING THE GREAT AND MOST PRECIOUS REVELATIONS NOW PRINTED FOR OUR GUIDE. I SAW HIM TRANSLATING BY INSPIRATION, THE OLD AND NEW TESTAMENTS, AND THE INSPIRED BOOK OF ABRAHAM FROM EGYPTIAN PAPYRUS." — *Orson Pratt*

shop, ashery, tannery, shoe shop, forge, pottery, steam sawmill, and lumber kiln—became thriving enterprises.

"The starting up, as if by magic, of buildings in every direction around us, were evincive to us of buoyant hope, lively anticipation, and a firm confidence that our days of pinching adversity had passed," wrote Oliver Cowdery.[21] To the amazement of near neighbors, Mormons turned Kirtland from a sleepy village into a mushrooming community that was larger, and some said more notable than the Ohio towns of Chardon, Painesville, Akron, Canton, Warren, and Youngstown.

Orchestrating the prosperity and its attendant unity was the Prophet Joseph Smith. To accomplish all that he had in his brief sojourn in Ohio, one observer concluded that he must surely be greater than man himself. Of the observer, Joseph wrote, "I was this morning introduced to a man from the east. After hearing my name, he remarked that I was nothing but a man, indicating by this expression, that he had supposed that a person to whom the Lord should see fit to reveal His will, must be something more than a man." John Hollister of Portage County, Ohio, did not think Joseph was more than a man. He was convinced that God had not revealed anything to the Prophet respecting his holy word. Joseph mused, "[Hollister] tarried overnight with me, and acknowledged in the morning that, although he had thought he knew something about religion, he was now sensible that he knew but little." The Prophet then added, "which was the greatest trait of wisdom I could discover in him."[22]

Joseph did not allow the words or actions of these men or any others to hamper him in setting forth the order of the Church. He called apostles, seventies, bishops, and stake presidents to administer the affairs of the kingdom. He established a school of the prophets for instruction of the priesthood that was to become "a sanctuary, a tabernacle of the Holy Spirit to [their] edification." He called elders to share the gospel throughout the United States, Canada, and England. He taught with power the laws of God and the steps necessary to enter his kingdom. He stated, "They are they who received the testimony of Jesus, and believed on his name and were baptized after the manner of his burial, being buried in the water in his name, and this according to the commandment which he

PAGE 46: *Morocco Chest used to store Bible Translation*
PAGE 47: *Bedroom in John Johnson Home in Hiram*

"A mob of about thirty people, stimulated by whiskey and disguised with colored faces, attacked Joseph Smith and Sidney Rigdon and tarred and feathered them." — *Geauga Gazette, April 17, 1832*

"Simonds, Simonds, where's the tar bucket? I don't know, answered one, where 'tis Eli's left it." —Joseph Smith
Recollections the night he was tarred and feathered

has given— ... And who overcome by faith and are sealed by the Holy Spirit of promise, which the Father sheds forth upon all those who are just and true." Truly, these were glorious days in Kirtland—days of learning from and heeding the words of the Lord's mouthpiece.

It was also a day for building "a house, even a house of prayer, a house of fasting, a house of faith, a house of learning, a house of glory, a house of order, a house of God."[23] One Latter-day Saint suggested to the Prophet a wood-framed structure would suffice. Another proposed a log structure. "Shall we, brethren, build a house for our God, of logs?" Joseph asked. "No," he retorted, "I have a better plan than that. I have a plan of the house of the Lord, given by himself."[24]

The Lord's plan for the Kirtland Temple was intricate and multifaceted in design and financially well beyond the means of the Latter-day Saints. "Notwithstanding the Church was poor," Joseph explained, and that "there was not a scraper and hardly a plow that could be found among the Saints," the followers of Joseph Smith willingly tackled the impossible.[25] John Tanner "loaned the prophet two thousand dollars" to secure the land on which the temple would be built.[26] On June 5, 1833, "George A. Smith hauled the first load of stone" from the quarry. Later, Hyrum Smith struck "the first blow upon the house."[27] By summer of 1833 nearly every Latter-day Saint in Kirtland had contributed in some way toward the building. Men cut stones,

PAGE 48 LEFT: *Memorial Window for Symonds Ryder at a church in Hiram* RIGHT: *Interior of John Johnson Home* PAGE 49: *School of the Prophets Room in the Newel K. Whitney and Co. Store in Kirtland*

"The Prophet Joseph started a school there for the brethren to learn the classical language but more especially Hebrew and had hired an efficient professional linguist for that purpose." — *George A. Smith*

"[WEDNESDAY, 16 DECEMBER 1835], RETURNED HOME, ELDER [MCCLELLAN], ELDER BRIGHAM YOUNG AND ELDER JARED CARTER CALLED AND PAID ME A VISIT WITH WHICH I WAS MUCH GRATIFIED." —Joseph Smith

fell trees, and donated carpentry skills. Their wives helped, too. Heber C. Kimball explained, "Our wives were all the time knitting, spinning and sewing, and, in fact, I may say doing all kinds of work! They were just as busy as any of us."[28] Among their number was Mother Smith. "There was but one main-spring to all our thoughts and actions," she penned, "and that was, the building of the Lord's house."[29]

Mobs in Kirtland attempted to stop Latter-day Saints from laboring on the rising temple walls, but to no avail. Mormon faithful not only put down the mob, but redoubled their efforts and prepared to defend the walls, themselves, and their prophet. "Our enemies were raging and threatening destruction upon us," Heber C. Kimball recalled. "[We] were obliged to lie with our fire-locks in our arms, to preserve Brother Joseph's life."[30] For what seemed like months, the faithful "gave no sleep to their eyes, nor slumber to their eyelids" to protect the Lord's House and his servant.[31]

Notwithstanding the threats, temple construction moved forward at an urgent pace until it's completion in March 1836. At the temple dedication on March 27, Joseph asked the Lord in prayer, "And we ask thee, Holy Father, that thy servants may go forth from this house armed with thy power, and that thy name may be upon them, and thy glory be round about them ... enable thy servants to seal up the law, and bind up the testimony."[32] Benjamin Brown testified that the prophetic plea was fulfilled that very day. "As on the day of Pentecost, [the Holy Ghost] was profusely poured out. Hundreds of Elders spoke in tongues," reported Brown. "We had a most glorious and never-to-be-forgotten time. Angels were seen by numbers present."[33] Convert William Draper added the Spirit of God entered the temple "like a mighty rushing wind and filled the house, that many that were present spoke in tongues and had visions and saw angels and prophesied."[34] Eliza R. Snow observed that "the ceremonies of that dedication may be rehearsed" as they were by Brown and Draper, "but no mortal language can describe the heavenly manifestations of that memorable day."[35]

One week later—on Easter morn and on the Jewish holy day of Passover—other epochal manifestations were seen in the holy house. "I retired to the pulpit, the veils being dropped, and bowed myself, with Oliver Cowdery, in solemn and silent prayer," Joseph wrote. While they were in silent prayer, "the veil was taken from our minds,

"And again, let my servant John Johnson have the house in which he lives, and the inheritance, all save the ground which has been reserved for the building of my houses."

—*Doctrine and Covenants 104:34*

and the eyes of our understanding were opened. We saw the Lord standing upon the breastwork of the pulpit, before us; and under his feet was a paved work of pure gold, in color like amber. His eyes were as a flame of fire; the hair of his head was white like the pure snow; his countenance shone above the brightness of the sun; and his voice was as the sound of the rushing of great waters, even the voice of Jehovah." The Savior said, "I have accepted this house.... And the fame of this house shall spread to foreign lands; and this is the beginning of the blessing which shall be poured out upon the heads of my people."[36]

Following the temple dedication and heavenly manifestations of the Savior, Moses, Elias, and Elijah, the Saints of Ohio experienced difficult days. The financial collapse of the Mormon bank, like many other banks during this time, was viewed as central to that difficulty. The bank's failure caused some Latter-day Saints to waver, reconsider their faith, then collapse, much like the bank. Benjamin Johnson lamented how quickly Latter-day Saints forget the sacred and succumb to apostasy. "Like Judas, [these men were] ready to sell or destroy the Prophet Joseph and his followers. And it almost seemed to me that the brightest stars in our firmament had fallen," he penned.[37]

As for the prophet, Joseph remained strong but sorrowful. To him, "it seemed as though all the powers of earth and hell were combining their influence in an especial manner to overthrow the Church at once, and make a final end."[38] To protect him and themselves from further apostate abuse, "every night for a long time [the faithful lay] upon our arms to keep off *mobs*, of forties, of eighties, & of hundreds to save our lives ... that we might not be scattered & driven to the four winds!"[39]

PAGE 50: *Joseph Smith Home in Kirtland* PAGE 51: *John Johnson Inn in Kirtland*

"I ACTED AS FOREMAN IN THE TEMPLE STONE QUARRY, AND WHEN OTHER DUTIES WOULD PERMIT, LABORED WITH MY OWN HANDS." —*Joseph Smith*

"During this siege of darkness [Brigham] stood close by Joseph.... [I] put forth my utmost energies to sustain the servant of God and unite the Quorums of the Church," he said.[40] Levi Hancock also supported the Prophet. "I did all I could to hold up that good man," Levi wrote. "My heart would ache for him. He had to stand against thousands of his pretended friends seeking to overthrow him. It was terrible the abuse he suffered."[41]

PAGE 52: *Temple Quarry* PAGES 52–53: *Exterior and Interior of Kirtland Temple*

"There was but one main spring to all our thoughts and actions, and that was, the building of the Lord's house." —*Lucy Mack Smith*

"We saw the Lord standing upon the breastwork of the pulpit, before us; and under his feet was a paved work of pure gold, in color like amber." — *Doctrine and Covenants 110:2*

Day of Temple Dedication "ALL THE CONGREGATION SIMULTANEOUSLY AROSE, BEING MOVED UPON BY AN INVISIBLE POWER; MANY BEGAN TO SPEAK IN TONGUES AND PROPHESY; OTHERS SAW GLORIOUS VISIONS; AND I BEHELD THE TEMPLE WAS FILLED WITH ANGELS, WHICH FACT I DECLARED TO THE CONGREGATION." —*Joseph Smith*

Yet all was not bad. Interspersed within the relentless persecution were tender moments in Joseph's life. One was the night he overhead a little boy praying for his safety from the menacing mob. After listening to the boy's humble prayer, Joseph told his friends "to go to bed and all sleep and rest themselves that night, for God had heard and would answer that boy's prayer."[42] They did as advised and none were disturbed or molested. Choice moments, however, proved too few and far between as abuse escalated. So violent did the mobs become that Joseph "regarded it as unsafe to remain any longer in Kirtland, and began to make arrangements to move to Missouri."[43]

PAGES 54–55: *Interior of Kirtland Temple*

"My grandmother [Mary Duty Smith] fell asleep without sickness, pain or regret. She breathed her last about sunset, and was buried in the burial ground near the Temple."—*Joseph Smith*

Making the same arrangements were those who refused to deny Joseph's prophetic calling. Their refusal was viewed as an affirmation for the lawless to destroy their belongings. As the mobs began to break into homes and steal provisions, some Latter-day Saints quailed under their threats and denounced their faith. Others would not no matter the consequences. Of them, Zadoc Judd said, "Apostates and mobbers had caused nearly all the good and worthy people to leave the place."[44] One who endured the abuse, packed his wagon, and moved onto Missouri was Benjamin Johnson. "With all my faults I did not forget the Lord nor His chosen servants," he penned. "And in this day of great affliction and separation by apostasy, I felt to call mightily upon His name, that He would never leave me to follow these examples, but that He would keep me humble, even though in poverty and affliction."[45] During these turbulent

"WE TURNED THE KEY AND LOCKED THE DOOR OF OUR HOMES, LEAVING OUR PROPERTY AND ALL WE POSSESSED IN THE HANDS OF ENEMIES AND STRANGERS." — *William F. Cahoon*

times those who endured queried, "What the Lord will do with us I know not, altho he slay me I will trust in him." John Smith believed, "We are like the ancients wandering from place to place in the wilderness."[46]

Among those seen taunting the Latter-day Saints and forcing their departure from Kirtland was Lyman Johnson, once a member of the Quorum of the Twelve Apostles. Years later he lamented his actions and said, "If I could believe 'Mormonism' as I did when I traveled with you and preached, if I possessed the world I would give it. I would give anything, I would suffer my right hand to be cut off, if I could believe it again. Then I was full of joy and gladness. My dreams were pleasant. When I awoke in the morning my spirit was cheerful. I was happy by day and by night, full of peace and joy and thanksgiving. But now it is darkness, pain, sorrow, misery in the extreme."[47]

In contrast to the regrets of Johnson were the feelings of Brigham Young. "I feel like shouting hallelujah, all the time, when I think that I ever knew Joseph Smith, the Prophet whom the Lord raised up and ordained, and to whom He gave keys and power to build up the kingdom of God on earth," he said.[48] Notwithstanding the scenes that he and others had passed through in Kirtland, they willingly followed their prophet to Missouri. They left behind family and friends who had made different choices. They also left behind a symbol of their faith, a House of the Lord—the Kirtland Temple.

PAGE 56 LEFT: *Tower on the Kirtland Temple* RIGHT: *Graveyard near the Kirtland Temple*
PAGE 57: *Warren Parish Home in Kirtland*

Plead Unto Heaven

CHAPTER THREE

PLEAD UNTO HEAVEN

"The Prophet's voice was like the thunders of heaven, yet his language was meek and his instructions edified much. There was a power and majesty that attended his words and preaching that we never beheld in any man before."

—Joseph L. Robinson[1]

The Saints of Ohio viewed their arrival in Missouri as a welcome respite from past cares. They were now in what Joseph Smith described as the "beautiful rolling prairies [that] lie spread out like a sea of meadows; and are decorated with a growth of flowers so gorgeous and grand as to exceed description."[2] In this idyllic setting, Mormon newcomers trusted that the tribulations of yesteryears were behind them and not a foretaste of what lay ahead. To them, Missouri was the promised Zion that the Lord holds in his hands. In Jackson County, Missouri, the Prophet Joseph had dedicated a temple site. And now this promised land bid them welcome.

Yet tales of prejudice and hatred stemming from the growth of Mormonism in Missouri sounded all too familiar to them. Edward Partridge bearing "abuse with so much resignation and meekness, that it appeared to astound the multitude, who permitted me to retire in silence, many looking very solemn, their sympathies having been touched," was reminiscent of scenes in Ohio.[3] Levi Hancock's words, "All my property was scattered to the four winds, tools and all for pretended claims, where I owed not one cent justly" resonated with events they had known in Kirtland.[4] And Joseph Knight's description of "submit[ting] to the numerous indignities heaped upon us,... [and] made many concessions to the mob in hope of pacifying them, but it was useless," sounded as if he had spoken these words in Ohio.[5]

"Would mobs assemble to drive them from these lands, too?" they asked. The answer alluded them for a time, but not long. There was much to accomplish in the months that lay ahead before violence would again overtake them. Joseph Smith warned his followers to stay alert

PAGES 58–59, 60: *Valley of Adam-ondi-Ahman*

"The country is unlike the timbered states of the East. As far as the eye can reach the beautiful rolling prairies lie spread out like a sea of meadows; and are decorated with a growth of flowers so gorgeous and grand as to exceed description." —*Joseph Smith*

and protect themselves as they worked the Missouri soil and built their homes for they were now living among "a ferocious set of mobbers, like lambs among wolves."[6] He counseled them to rise above retaliation for past and future wrongs and build up the communities of Far West, DeWitt, and Adam-ondi-Ahman in spite of outward challenges. The Saints listened and obeyed.

They transformed rolling Missouri prairies into enterprising communities. Shops, mercantile establishments, and hundreds of log homes were the fruits of their labors. Their log structures evidenced a growing hope that this was a new day for the faithful—a day free from harassment and persecution—a day when mobocracy was no where to be found. But such hopes did not last long. Disaffected Ohio apostates journeyed to Missouri to "contaminate the minds of many of the brethren against Joseph, in order to destroy his influence."[7] Oliver Cowdery and David Whitmer were but two who listened to them. "Give me my freedom or take my life!" cried Cowdery. "I shall no longer be bound by the chains of hell. I shall speak out when I see a move to deceive the ignorant."[8] His cries were followed by Whitmer's assertion that Joseph Smith had "abandon[ed] the primitive faith" and the Saints who stood by him would "drift into error and spiritual blindness."[9]

"THE PLACE WHICH IS NOW CALLED INDEPENDENCE IS THE CENTER PLACE; AND A SPOT FOR THE TEMPLE IS LYING WESTWARD, UPON A LOT WHICH IS NOT FAR FROM THE COURTHOUSE."

— *Doctrine and Covenants 57:3*

Apostate lies from once close friends did not alter Joseph's course or cause him to falter. The acidic words that beckoned the elect of God to choose evil did not sway his resolve to choose good. He continued to share the gospel of Jesus Christ with all who would listen. He called upon the faithful to do the same. He began writing the history of the Church and announced plans for building the Far West Temple. He established a settlement and stake at Adam-ondi-Ahman and received a revelation commanding the payment of tithes on interest.

Joseph's unruffled demeanor amid harassment, vexatious law suits, and falsehoods aplenty gave evidence that nothing the apostates said or did could thwart him from his chosen course. Frustrated by their failings and needing support to bolster their case against the Latter-day Saint Prophet, the turncoats sent an affidavit to Missouri Governor Lilburn W. Boggs claiming that Joseph Smith was a modern Mohammed and that he was arming Native Americans with explosive weapons that could destroy law and order in the state. Although the affidavit was utterly false, the governor acted upon the charges with a swiftness of executive power that surprised even the apostates. On October 27, 1838, Governor Boggs issued an extermination order against Later-day Saints living in Missouri. "The Mormons must be treated as enemies and must be exterminated or driven from the state, if necessary for the public good," the order read. The Mormon "outrages are beyond all description," the governor penned.[10]

A massacre in the Mormon community of Haun's Mill and the fall of DeWitt stemmed from the governmental decree. Hyrum Smith "endeavored to find out for what cause" the Latter-day Saints were subjected to such violence and even death. "All we could learn was, that it was because we were 'Mormons,'" said Hyrum. "We have been driven time after time, and without cause; and smitten again and again, and that without provocation," was Joseph's response.[11] But this time the abuse was unprecedented. The executive government sanctioned order literally put in harm's way every man, woman, and child who would not deny that Joseph Smith was a Prophet.

Fearful Latter-day Saints scattered, hoping to save their lives and find safety beyond the borders of Missouri. Those who could not escape to the state borders ran to Far West, the center of the Mormon communities in Missouri. Instead of finding Far West a bastion of safety for them, they found the community encircled by citizen/soldier militias bent on carrying out the governor's extermination order.

PAGE 62: *Temple Block in Independence* PAGE 63: *James Flourney Home near Temple Block*

"LET MY SERVANT SIDNEY GILBERT PLANT HIMSELF IN THIS PLACE, AND ESTABLISH A STORE, THAT HE MAY SELL GOODS WITHOUT FRAUD, THAT HE MAY OBTAIN MONEY TO BUY LANDS FOR THE GOOD OF THE SAINTS."

— *Doctrine and Covenants 57:8*

Trusting that extermination could be avoided, Joseph and his closest associates ventured outside the confines of Far West to speak with the military generals stationed on the periphery of the town waiting for orders to attack. This venture proved ill-advised. As Parley P. Pratt wrote, "We had no confidence in the word" of the military leaders. But believing themselves with "no alternative but to put ourselves into the hands of such monsters, or to have the city attacked, and men, women and children massacred," Joseph and his brother Hyrum Smith, Parley P. Pratt, Sidney Rigdon, and other Latter-day Saint leaders "commended [them]selves to the Lord, and voluntarily surrendered as sheep into the hands of wolves."[12]

When news of their surrender passed from man to man in the military encampment, enthusiastic soldiers quickly discarded military decorum and yelled like lawless mobbers or as "so many bloodhounds let loose upon their prey ... Had the army been composed of so many bloodhounds, wolves, and panthers, they could not have made a sound more terrible," wrote Pratt. "If the vision of the infernal regions could suddenly open to the mind, with thousands of malicious fiends, all clamoring ... raging and foaming like a troubled sea, then could some idea be formed of the hell which we had entered."[13]

PAGE 64: *Gilbert and Whitney Store in Independence*
PAGE 65: *Missouri River*

"For I, the Lord, have decreed in mine anger many destructions upon the waters; yea, and especially upon these waters. Nevertheless, all flesh is in mine hand, and he that is faithful among you shall not perish by the waters." — *Doctrine and Covenants 61:5–6*

"[We] could distinctly hear their horrid yellings," said Mother Smith of that late October night in 1838 at Far West. "Not knowing the cause, we supposed they were murdering [Joseph]." Father Smith sobbed, "Oh, my God! my God! they have killed my son! they have murdered him! and I must die, for I cannot live without him!" He then "fell back upon [the bed] helpless as a child."[14]

During the long evening hours that followed, military guards "kept up a constant tirade of mockery, and the most obscene blackguardism and abuse. They blasphemed God; mocked Jesus Christ; swore the most dreadful oaths; taunted brother Joseph and others; demanded miracles; wanted signs, such as: 'Come, Mr. Smith, show us an angel.' 'Give us one of your revelations.' 'Show us a miracle.'...'Or, if you are Apostles or men of God, deliver yourselves, and then we will be Mormons.'"[15] In answer to the mockery, Joseph and the Mormon captives fell silent. The danger in which they now found themselves demanded their quiet attention, not verbal expressions of fear.

While the prisoners awaited word of their fate outside of Far West, a military tribunal convened under the leadership of General Samuel Lucas. The avowed purpose of the tribunal was to determine whether the prisoners should be permitted to live or die. Officers, local ministers,

"WE WRAPPED HIM [JESSE SMITH] UP IN HIS BED-CLOTHES AND CARRIED HIM AND THE OTHER BRETHREN THAT HAD DIED, AND PUT THEM IN GRAVES THAT HAD BEEN DUG FOR THEM. WE CARRIED THEM THROUGH A TERRIBLE THUNDER-STORM; WE LAID THEM IN THEIR GRAVES WITHOUT ANY COFFINS AND COVERED THEM WITH MOTHER EARTH." —*James Henry Rollins*

and judges demanded the lives of the prisoners be forfeited. Only one man in the tribunal expressed views to the contrary. "The age of extermination was over," announced General Alexander Doniphan. He stood in defense of the Mormon prisoners arguing that these men "had never belonged to any lawful military organization and could not therefore have violated military law." He further argued that the assembled court martial was "illegal as hell."[16] In spite of his plausible arguments, the prisoners were condemned to death and General Doniphan ordered to carry out the execution.

Sir: *You will take Joseph Smith and the other prisoners into the public square of Far West, and shoot them at 9 o'clock to-morrow morning.*

SAMUEL D. LUCAS, Major-General Commanding.

Doniphan replied to General Lucas,

It is cold-blooded murder. I will not obey your order. My brigade shall march for Liberty tomorrow morning, at 8 o'clock; and if you execute these men, I will hold you responsible before an earthly tribunal, so help me God!

A.W. DONIPHAN, Brigadier-General.[17]

"One night the snow fell four or five inches. The Prophet, seeing our forlorn condition, called on us to form into two parties—Lyman Wight at the head of one line and he (Joseph) heading the other line—to have a sham battle. The weapons were snowballs. We set to with a will full of glee and fun." — *Edward Stevenson*

Privately Doniphan told General Lucas, "You hurt one of these men if you dare and I will hold you personally responsible for it, and at some other time you and I will meet again when in mortal combat and we will see who is the better man."[18] Fearing the retribution of Doniphan, Lucas dared not execute the prisoners that day. Seeking an alternative that would not demean him in front of his soldiers, Lucas determined to take the prisoners to his hometown of Independence, Missouri, and "show them off."

Mormon captives were ordered to climb inside wagons for the journey that lay ahead. One prisoner requested the right to gather food and clothing from his home in Far West. Reluctantly, his request was granted and opened the way for all prisoners to return for necessities to Far West before the journey. Prisoner wagons rolled through Far West at an early hour on the morning of November 1, 1838. When one wagon stopped in front of Joseph's home, a guard of six soldiers escorted him inside. "Father, is the mob going to kill you?" Joseph's young son asked. "You d— little brat, go back; you will see your father no more," was a guard's retort.[19] After obtaining necessary food and clothing, the Latter-day Saint Prophet was forced back into the wagon and a tarp was then affixed to the wagon preventing near neighbors, who now rushed toward the scene, from communicating with him.

Among those who hurried toward the wagon was Mother Smith. "I am the mother of the Prophet—is there not a gentleman here, who will assist me to that wagon, that I may take a last look at my children, and speak to them once more before I die?" she asked. A man assisted her to reach the wagon. "Mr. Smith, your mother and sister are here, and wish to shake hands with you," spoke the man. Joseph responded by thrusting his hand through the tarp. "Joseph, do speak to your poor mother once more—I cannot bear to go till I hear your voice." The words "God bless you, mother!" were spoken.[20] The well guarded wagons then rolled out of Far West.

PAGE 66: *Fishing River* PAGE 67: *Memorial Marker for Zion's Camp in Independence*

"We lived in tents until winter set in, and did our cooking out in the wind and storms. Log heaps were our parlor stoves, and the cold, wet ground our velvet carpets, and the crying of little children our piano forte."

— Emily Austin

"Be of good cheer, brethren," Joseph said to fellow captives. "The word of the Lord came to me last night that our lives should be given us, and that whatever we may suffer during this captivity, not one of our lives should be taken."[21] The prisoners were comforted by his words but not free from the trials and mockery that lay on the road ahead. "Which of the prisoners [is] the Lord whom the 'Mormons' worship?" a woman sarcastically asked as the wagons stopped in her town. A soldier pointed to Joseph. She asked him "whether [he] professed to be the Lord and Savior?" Joseph replied, "I profess to be nothing but a man, and a minister of salvation, sent by Jesus Christ to preach the Gospel."[22] He then taught her the basic doctrines of the kingdom—faith, repentance, and baptism. "All seemed surprised, and the lady, in tears, went her way, praising God for the truth, and praying aloud that the Lord would bless and deliver the prisoners."[23]

An answer to her prayer was slow in coming. A jail in Independence awaited the prisoners. Under the scrutiny of prison guards "hundreds flocked to see us day after

PAGE 68: *Log Heaps on Shoal Creek at Haun's Mill*
PAGE 69: *Presumed Charles C. Rich Cabin in Far West*

"My husband had built a nice little hewed log house and made it ready to live in by the time we were married. It was four miles from Far West near my husband's father's [home]." — *Sarah Rich*

day" in the Independence jail, Pratt recalled. "We spent most of our time in preaching and conversation, explanatory of our doctrines and practice. Much prejudice was removed, and the feelings of the populace began to be in our favor, notwithstanding their former wickedness and hatred."[24] The prisoners were next conveyed under guard to Richmond a few miles distance. There, the captives were incarcerated in a small log house and shackled with irons. To his wife, Joseph penned, "My Dear Emma, we are prisoners in chains, and under strong guards, for Christ['s] sake and for no other cause.... Brother Robinson is chained, next to me he has a true heart and a firm mind, Brother Wight, is next, Br. Rigdon, next, Hyrum, next, Parely, next Amasa, next, and thus we are bound together in chains as well as the cords of everlasting love.... We are in good spirits and rejoice that we are counted worthy to be persecuted for Christ['s] sake."[25]

As the Latter-day Saint leaders waited for a court hearing to determine the cause for holding them in jail, they were forced to listen to unfeeling guards recount the atrocities committed in Far West upon Mormons in the name of the extermination order. 'I had listened till I became so disgusted, shocked, horrified, and so filled with the spirit of indignant justice that I could scarcely refrain from rising upon my feet

"THEREFORE, I COMMAND YOU TO BUILD A HOUSE UNTO ME, FOR THE GATHERING TOGETHER OF MY SAINTS THAT THEY MAY WORSHIP ME." — *Doctrine and Covenants 115:8*

and rebuking the guards," wrote Pratt. Joseph felt no such restraints. "He stood erect in terrible majesty. Chained, and without a weapon; calm, unruffled and dignified [and] ... spoke in a voice of thunder, or as the roaring lion ...: 'SILENCE, ye fiends of the infernal pit. In the name of Jesus Christ I rebuke you, and command you to be still; I will not live another minute and hear such language. Cease such talk, or you or I die THIS INSTANT!'" The guards quailed before him and "lowered or dropped" their weapons to the ground. Their "knees smote together, and who, shrinking into a corner, or crouching at his feet, begged his pardon, and remained quiet till a change of guards."[26]

Following this scene, a few days later a civil hearing began to determine if the state had just cause to keep the Mormon leaders confined. The courtroom filled to capacity with those who prided themselves on being Mormon haters. "There is a red hot Mormon, d-m him, I am acquainted with him," shouted one man. Another yelled, "Shoot your Mormon, I have shot mine."[27] The Presiding Judge Austin King failed to stop the outbursts, in fact, he seemed pleased.

By the end of the first day of the civil hearing, Joseph was confident that "on examination, I think that the authorities, will discover our innocence, and set us free."[27] As the days of the hearing extended to

"[JOSEPH] TOOK HEAVEN,
FIGURATIVELY SPEAKING,
AND BROUGHT IT DOWN TO EARTH;
AND HE TOOK THE EARTH,
BROUGHT IT UP, AND OPENED UP,
IN PLAINNESS AND SIMPLICITY,
THE THINGS OF GOD."
— *Brigham Young*

fourteen, his confidence waned for apostate witnesses had committed perjury to prove old rumors and fabricate new ones against the captives."Renegade 'Mormon' dissenters are... spreading various foul and libelous reports against us, thinking thereby to gain the friendship of the world," said Joseph. "We have waded through an ocean of tribulation and mean abuse, practiced upon us by the ill bred and the ignorant."[28]

Judge King was one of the ignorant. After eliciting a testimony from Joseph about the Old Testament prophet Daniel's interpretation of Nebuchadnezzar's dream (about the stone cut out of the mountain), he turned to his clerk and said, "Write that down; it is a strong point for treason." Joseph's defense attorney, Alexander Doniphan, objected to such courtroom irregularity but was overruled. Angered by the ruling, Doniphan retorted, "Judge, you had better make the Bible treason."[29]

As the hearing drew to a close, Judge King ordered six Mormon prisoners, including the Prophet Joseph, to go to Liberty Jail on charges of overt treason. Outraged by the ruling, Doniphan said, "If a cohort

PAGE 70: *Temple Site in Far West*
PAGE 71: *Sunrise near Far West*

"Brother Daniel, it is about two years since I have written you; ... We are about nineteen-hundred miles apart yet the same sun shines on you that does on me ... Mormonism so-called has not come to naught ... it is like the stone that Daniel saw that was cut out of the mountain without hands that filled the whole earth." —*James Aldrich*

"Spring Hill is named by the Lord Adam-ondi-Ahman, because, said he, it is the place where Adam shall visit his people, or the Ancient of Days shall sit, as spoken of by Daniel the Prophet." — *Doctrine and Covenants 116*

"This earth was once a garden place,
With all her glories common,
And men did live a holy race,
And worship Jesus face to face,
In Adam-ondi-Ahman.

Hosanna to such days to come,
The Savior's second coming,
When all the earth in glorious bloom
Affords the Saints a holy home,
Like Adam-ondi-Ahman."

— *William W. Phelps*

of angels were to come down, and declare [the prisoners] innocent, it would all be the same; for [King] had determined from the beginning to cast [them] into prison."[30] Joseph declared, "There was not the least shadow of honor, or justice, or law, administered toward them, but sheer prejudice, and the spirit of persecution and malice."[31]

On December 1, 1838, six Mormon prisoners were incarcerated in Liberty Jail. "Our place of lodging was the square side of hewed white oak logs, and our food was anything but good and decent," wrote Hyrum Smith. "Poison was administered to us three or four times.... The poison would inevitably have proved fatal had not the power of Jehovah interposed in our behalf, to save us from their wicked purpose." Two petitions addressed to the highest court in Missouri asking for a writ of habeas corpus for the prisoners were denied. Unofficially, the reason given was that "there was no law

PAGES 72–75: *Valley of Adam-ondi-Ahman*

"The mob went towards [Adam-ondi-Ahman in] Daviess county, and while on their way there they took two of our men prisoners, and made them ride upon the cannon, and told them, that they would drive the 'Mormons' from Daviess to Caldwell, and from Caldwell to hell."

— *Memorial sent to Missouri State Legislature, Hosea Stout, Recorder, January 30, 1843*

"The banks of Shoal creek on either side teemed with children sporting and playing, while their mothers were engaged in domestic employments, and their fathers employed in guarding the mills and other property." — *Joseph Young Sr.*

"My husband was shot in the neck where it cut off all feeling of his body. It is of no use for me to try and tell how I felt for that is impossible, but I could not have shed a tear if all had been dead before me. I went to work to try and get my husband warm, but could not." — *Drusilla Hendricks*

"YET THOUGH WE WERE WOMEN,
WITH TENDER CHILDREN,
IN FLIGHT FOR OUR LIVES,
THE DEMONS POURED VOLLEY
AFTER VOLLEY TO KILL US."
— *Amanda Barnes Smith*

for the Mormons in the State of Missouri."[32] Why the continued abuse? Joseph believed it stemmed from hatred. "The soldiers and officers of every kind hated us, and the most profane blasphemers and drunkards & whoremongers hated us," he wrote. "They all hated us most cordially. And now what did they hate us for, purely because of the testimony of Jesus Christ."[33]

At a time when hope seemed darkest in Liberty Jail, Joseph wrote optimistic letters to Emma and the Saints who had escaped from Missouri and were clustering in Quincy, Illinois. To Emma, he penned, "As to yourself if you want to know how much I want to see you, examine your feelings, how much you want to see me, and Judge for yourself, I would gladly walk from here to you barefoot, and bareheaded, and half naked, to see you and think it great pleasure, and never count it toil."[34] To the Saints in Quincy, he wrote of his confidence in the Lord, "What power shall stay the heavens? As well might man stretch forth his puny arm to stop the Missouri river in its decreed course, or to turn it up stream, as to hinder the Almighty from pouring down knowledge from heaven upon the heads of the Latter-day Saints."[35]

For himself and fellow Mormon captives, he now asked, "O God, where art thou? And where is the

PAGE 76 TOP: *Shoal Creek near Haun's Mill* BOTTOM: *Crooked River*
PAGE 77: *Millstone Marker near Haun's Mill*

"I WILL NOT OBEY YOUR ORDER....
IF YOU EXECUTE THESE MEN,
I WILL HOLD YOU RESPONSIBLE
BEFORE AN EARTHLY TRIBUNAL,
SO HELP ME GOD."
— *Alexander Doniphan*

pavilion that covereth thy hiding place? How long shall thy hand be stayed, and thine eye, yea thy pure eye, behold from the eternal heavens the wrongs of thy people and of thy servants, and thine ear be penetrated with their cries?" Answering the prophetic plea, the Lord assured his prophet, "My son, peace be unto thy soul; thine adversity and thine afflictions shall be but a small moment; And then, if thou endure it well, God shall exalt thee on high; thou shalt triumph over all thy foes. Thy friends do stand by thee, and they shall hail thee again with warm hearts and friendly hands. Thou art not yet as Job; thy friends do not contend against thee, neither charge thee with transgression, as they did Job.... If the very jaws of hell shall gape open the mouth wide after thee, know thou, my son, that all these things shall give thee experience, and shall be for thy good. The Son of Man hath descended below them all. Art thou greater than he? ... The ends of the earth shall inquire after thy name.... Fear not what man can do, for God shall be with you forever and ever."[36]

The hand of providence was soon revealed in the lives of Joseph and fellow prisoners. It was best seen in their escape from prison guards. In April 1839 the Mormon captives were being taken under guard to Columbia,

PAGE 78: *Alexander Doniphan Monument in Richmond*
PAGE 79 LEFT: *Tombstone of Judge Austin King in Richmond*
RIGHT: *Log Courthouse in Independence*

"[Joseph was] confined in a loathsome prison for no other cause or reason than that he claimed to be inspired of God to establish His church among men." — *Mercy Fielding Thompson*

"Not one charge could be substantiated against him. He was pure, just and holy as to the keeping of the law."
— *Brigham Young*

"WE ARE KEPT UNDER A STRONG GUARD, NIGHT AND DAY, IN A PRISON OF DOUBLE WALLS AND DOORS.... WE HAVE BEEN COMPELLED TO SLEEP ON THE FLOOR WITH STRAW, AND NOT BLANKETS SUFFICIENT TO KEEP US WARM; AND WHEN WE HAVE A FIRE, WE ARE OBLIGED TO HAVE ALMOST A CONSTANT SMOKE."

— *Joseph Smith*

Missouri, where they were to await a formal hearing on their alleged crimes. On the journey toward Columbia, their guards became visibly intoxicated. Ceasing the moment, the Mormon prisoners "took our change of venue for the state of Illinois."[37] Near the Mississippi River in the state of Illinois, Joseph reached safety and freedom. Hundreds of faithful Latter-day Saints were there to embrace him. Yet it was the embrace of fellow prisoner Parley P. Pratt that best bespeaks the moment: "Neither of us could refrain from tears as we embraced each other once more as free men," penned Pratt. "We felt like shouting hosannah in the highest, and giving glory to that God who had delivered us in fulfillment of His word."[38]

PAGE 80: *Liberty Jail (restored)* PAGE 81: *Mississippi River*

"No one but God, knows the reflections of my mind and the feelings of my heart when I left our house and home, and almost all of everything that we possessed excepting our little children, and took my journey out of the State of Missouri, leaving [my husband] shut up in that lonesome prison." — *Emma Smith*

Plead Unto Heaven

"THE MISSISSIPPI HAS AT LAST BROKEN ITS ICY BONDS, AND FLOWS MAJESTICALLY ONWARD, BLUE AND CLEAR AS CRYSTAL."

— *Charlotte Haven*

of Israel's God burning in my bosom, I forsook my home."[15] She, like others, came to leave a legacy—an imprint on the temple. The architect with his sand shaker box and the laborer with a chisel or wedge in hand were seen working daily on the temple site. Those carrying gauging tools, turning pegs, wooden mallets, and block planes commonly shared their expertise with novices. No one with a willing heart and a capacity for work was turned away, not even those who lacked tools.

In return for their labors, great blessings were promised. Blessings of eternity that would unite the laborers and their loved ones forever were to be received within the temple's finished walls. When some grew despondent with the slow process of placing one stone upon another, Joseph would say, "Brethren, shall we not go on in so great a cause? Go forward and not backward. Courage, brethren; and on, on to the victory! Let your hearts rejoice, and be exceedingly glad."[16]

"I could lean back and listen [to the Prophet]. Ah what pleasure this gave me," penned Wandle Mace. "He would unravel the scriptures and explain doctrine as no other man could. What had been mystery he made so plain it was no longer mystery.... I ask, who understood anything about these things until Joseph being inspired from on high touched the key and unlocked the door of these mysteries of the kingdom?"[17] During these gospel conversations, Joseph Smith explained the covenants and

PAGE 88: *Tombstones in the Old Nauvoo Burial Grounds*
PAGE 89: *Drainage Ditch in Nauvoo*

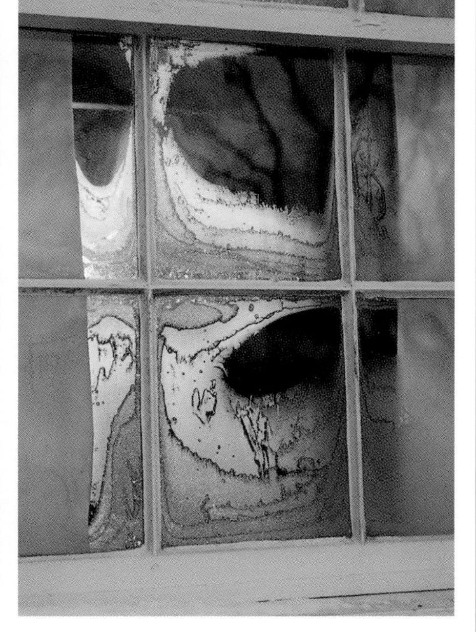

ordinances made in holy temples. He assured his followers that through participating in temple ordinances they would become more committed to a Christlike life and have a greater love for God. He taught, "The pleasing joys of family ties and associations contribute to the happiness, power and dominion of those who attain to the celestial glory."[18]

Though building the Nauvoo Temple was a labor of love and the occasion for a gospel discussion, its economic cost drained the resources of the emerging community of Nauvoo. "Some say it is better to give to the poor than build the Temple," said Joseph Smith, but he countered "the building of the Temple has sustained the poor who were driven from Missouri and kept them from starving; and it has been the best means of this object which could be devised."[19] To console those struggling with economic hardship, Joseph promised that they would be among the first to enter the holy temple.

Encouraged by his promise, men redoubled their efforts to finish the exterior walls. Their sacrifice was duly noted, but what brought acclaim from friend and foe alike was the unique edifice they were constructing. Jacob Scott penned, "The Temple exceeds in splendor and magnificence any building I have ever seen." Another visitor noted, "It was a large and splendid edifice, built on the Egyptian style

"THE BUILDINGS, THOUGH MANY OF THEM WERE SMALL AND OF WOOD, YET BORE THE MARKS OF NEATNESS WHICH I HAVE NOT SEEN EQUALLED IN THIS COUNTRY."

—*Reverend Samuel Prior*

"I remember Brother Joseph as he addressed an assembly of Saints, in the spring of 1844. It was under some large oak trees, in a hollow south of the temple, near to Parley street. He was discoursing upon the fact that God, in establishing His Church, had provided that only one man was authorized, of God, to receive revelations that should be binding upon the Church."

—*Angus M. Cannon*

of architecture, and its grandeur and magnificence truly astonished me."[20] With a sword in one hand and a trowel in the other, Joseph and his people were building an edifice to glorify God, and unknowingly, a memorial of their unwavering testimony.

From the foundation stones to the symbolic angel atop the tall spire, the laborers were building as they lived—steadfast and immovable. When harassment and persecution threatened them on every side in winter 1843-44, workers on the temple walls continued to build. When caustic newspaper editorials turned public

PAGE 90: *Block House in Nauvoo* PAGE 91: *Nauvoo Grove*

"[Joseph] was strong and active, and could build more rods of good fence in one day than most men could do in two, and he always left his fence clear of everything that might gather fire, such as underbrush, loose limbs, and tall strong weeds." —*Jesse W. Crosby*

"I HEARD HIM PREACH A NUMBER OF TIMES AND SAW HIM IN AND AROUND THE CITY, GIVING COUNSEL, AND I ALWAYS BELIEVED IN HIM FROM MY FIRST SEEING HIM UNTIL HIS DEATH, THAT HE WAS THE LEADER OF THIS DISPENSATION AND GOD ALMIGHTY'S PROPHET." — *William C. Staines*

sentiment from the rising temple walls to failings in the character and teachings of the Prophet Joseph, faithful Latter-day Saints kept building. When calls for Joseph's death grew loud and editor Thomas Sharp of the *Warsaw Signal* trumpeted, "Joe Smith is not safe out of Nauvoo. We would not be surprised to hear of his death by violent means in a short time," Latter-day Saints remained firm in their convictions and continued to build.[21]

Yet no one could deny that the peaceful co-existence of Nauvoo was threatened that winter. Leaders of neighboring communities, jealous of the emerging city, its temple, and its growing prosperity, threatened violence against all Latter-day Saints residing in Nauvoo if they did not abandon their holdings and leave the state. Editor Thomas Sharp predicted, "War and extermination is inevitable! CITIZENS ARISE, ONE AND ALL!!! Can you stand by, and suffer such INFERNAL DEVILS! to rob men of their property and RIGHTS, without avenging them. We have no time for comment; every man will make his own. LET IT BE MADE WITH POWDER AND BALL!!!"[22]

It was then that faithful Mormons left their positions on the temple walls and prepared to defend themselves, their Prophet, and their city. Only a few turncoats living inside of Nauvoo joined with those calling for extermination. These men pledged to murder the Latter-day Saint Prophet: "You solemnly swear, before God and all holy angels, and these your brethren by whom you are surrounded, that you will give your life, your liberty, your

PAGES 92-93: *Printing Office, John Taylor Home, Post Office in Nauvoo (restored)*

"THE SEVENTY ARE ALSO CALLED TO PREACH THE GOSPEL, AND TO BE ESPECIAL WITNESSES UNTO THE GENTILES AND IN ALL THE WORLD."

— *Doctrine and Covenants 107:25*

influence, your all, for the destruction of Joseph Smith and his party, so help you God!"[23] A signed affirmative oath bound the apostates in a satanic web.

Despite the threat from without and within, Nauvoo's leading citizen, Joseph Smith, was calm. "I do not regard my own life. I am ready to be offered a sacrifice for this people; for what can our enemies do? Only kill the body, and their power is then at an end," said Joseph.[24] His calm resolve was tested in June 1844. Apostates openly divulged their intent to destroy him and the church he had organized in the *Nauvoo Expositor*. Swift action by the Nauvoo city council declaring the *Expositor* a public nuisance led to the paper's destruction. The oath-bound publishers, seizing the opportunity to bring charges against Nauvoo public officials, like Joseph Smith, fled to Carthage. In that small community, public sentiment against the Mormons had been raised to a feverish pitch. Joseph was arrested and discharged twice for charges stemming from the destruction of the *Nauvoo Expositor*. The legal process, however, did not pacify his enemies. They clamored for blood. Despite their threats of murder, Joseph Smith confidently stated, "God Almighty is my shield; and what can man do if God is my friend? I shall not be sacrificed until my time comes; then shall I be offered freely."[25]

The Prophet made an attempt to escape the martyr's fate, but was thwarted when ill-advised friends asked him to give himself up to the law ascribed in Carthage. With resignation he uttered, "If my life is of no value to my

PAGE 94: *Seventies Hall in Nauvoo* PAGE 95 LEFT: *Cultural Hall in Nauvoo* RIGHT: *Scovil Bakery in Nauvoo*

"MR. EDITOR, TAKING IT AS IT IS, I WOULD ASK WHERE WE ARE TO GO FOR MUSIC, IF WE DO NOT FIND IT IN NAUVOO? I WILL BOLDLY ASSERT NO WHERE. WITNESS THE CONCERT THE OTHER EVENING AT THE MASONIC HALL; GOT UP FOR THE MOST LAUDABLE AND PRAISEWORTHY PURPOSE." — *Nauvoo Neighbor, October 30, 1844*

friends it is of none to myself." Following that resolve, early on Monday morning June 24 1844, the Prophet and his brother Hyrum began their journey to Carthage. As Joseph stopped to look upon the beautiful city that he had so carefully orchestrated he said, "This is the loveliest place and the best people under the heavens; little do they know the trials that await them."[26] To friend Dan Jones he confessed, "I love the city of Nauvoo too well to save my life at your expense. If I go not to them [Carthage], they will come and act out the horrid Missouri scenes in Nauvoo. I may prevent it. I fear not death. My work is well nigh done. Keep the faith and I will die for Nauvoo."[27]

"N.B. MARRIAGE CAKES MADE TO ORDER ON THE SHORTEST NOTICE FROM ONE TO TWENTY-FIVE DOLLARS EACH. L.N.S. NAUVOO DEC. 27, 1843." — *Nauvoo Neighbor, January 10, 1844*

"In the history of the whole world there cannot be found such another instance of so rapid a rise of a city out of the wilderness—a city so well built, a territory so well cultivated." —*J. H. Buckingham*

"The popular institutions of the day should not be our guide—that as daughters of Zion, we should set an example for all the world." — *Eliza R. Snow*

"Joseph Smith attended one of our Relief Society meetings in the lodge room. He opened the meeting by prayer. His voice trembled very much, after which he addressed us." — *Bathsheba W. Smith*

"[JOSEPH] SPENT DAY AFTER DAY, WEEK AFTER WEEK AND MONTH AFTER MONTH, TEACHING [THE TWELVE] AND A FEW OTHERS THE THINGS OF THE KINGDOM OF GOD." — *Wilford Woodruff*

For Joseph and Hyrum Smith, Carthage held little hope. Illegal court proceedings and incarceration on trumped up charges was their lot. From their room in the Carthage Jail, they heard the mob sing:

Where now is the Prophet Joseph?
Where now is the Prophet Joseph?
Where now is the Prophet Joseph?
Safe in Carthage jail![28]

"Could my brother Hyrum but be liberated," the Prophet wistfully mused, "it would not matter so much about me." To his wife Emma he confided, "I am very much resigned to my lot, knowing I am justified, and have done the best that could be done. Give my love to the children and all my friends."[29]

During the morning hours of June 27, 1844, Joseph and his brother Hyrum were visited by many friends. In the early afternoon their only visitors were two members of the Quorum of the Twelve—John Taylor and Willard Richards. John was asked to sing a hymn that seemed to harmonize with the sentiments of the jail scene:

In pris'n I saw him next, condemned
To meet a traitor's doom at morn.
The tide of lying tongues I stemmed,
And honored him 'mid shame and scorn.

My friendship's utmost zeal to try,
He asked if I for him would die.
The flesh was weak; my blood ran chill,
But my free spirit cried, "I will!"[30]

Around five o'clock in the afternoon "an armed mob—painted black—of from 150 to 200 persons" surrounded

PAGE 96 LEFT: *Nauvoo House in Nauvoo* RIGHT: *Sarah Granger Kimball Home in Nauvoo* PAGE 97: *Joseph Smith Jr. Brick Store in Nauvoo* PAGE 98: *Brigham Young House in Nauvoo* PAGE 99: *Exterior and Interior of Mansion House in Nauvoo*

"MY HOUSE HAS BEEN A HOME AND RESTING-PLACE FOR THOUSANDS, AND MY FAMILY MANY TIMES OBLIGED TO DO WITHOUT FOOD, AFTER HAVING FED ALL THEY HAD TO VISITORS." —*Joseph Smith*

the jail. Despite early attempts to defend themselves from lawless violence, the four men could not stop the brutal assassins. Hyrum Smith was the first to fall from an assassin's bullet. He fell to the ground exclaiming, "I am a dead man!"[31] Upon seeing him fall, Joseph sobbed, "Oh dear, brother Hyrum!"[32] Joseph then stepped toward the bedroom window. As he did so bullets shot from the door-way struck him as did two shot from outside. He fell from the window to the ground below after exclaiming, "O Lord, My God!"[33]

The workers of destruction left more than the corpses of two men. They left "a broad seal affixed to 'Mormonism' that cannot be rejected by any court on earth,... [and] truth of the everlasting gospel that all the world cannot impeach."[34] They left two martyr's crowns that they helped forge with their senseless brutality.

Of this brutality, John Taylor penned, "I felt a dull, lonely, sickening sensation at the news [of their deaths]. When I reflected that our noble chieftain, the Prophet of the living God, had fallen, and that I had seen his

"THE SAINTS HAVE THE PRIVILEGE OF BEING BAPTIZED FOR THOSE OF THEIR RELATIVES WHO ARE DEAD, WHOM THEY BELIEVE WOULD HAVE EMBRACED THE GOSPEL." —*Joseph Smith*

brother in the cold embrace of death, it seemed as though there was a void or vacuum in the great field of human existence to me, and a dark gloomy chasm in the kingdom, and that we were left alone."[35] Vilate Kimball wrote of the sorrow in Nauvoo, "Yea, every heart is filled with sorrow, and the very streets of Nauvoo seem to mourn. Where it will end the Lord only knows."[36] Newel Knight lamented, "O how I loved those men, and rejoiced under their teachings! It seems as if all is gone, and as if my heart strings will break, and were it not for my beloved wife and dear children I feel as if I have nothing to live for."[37]

The next morning, the corpses were transported from Carthage back to Nauvoo. Although thousands would view the remains of

PAGE 100 LEFT: *Baptism site on the Mississippi River* RIGHT: *Limestone Quarry in Nauvoo* PAGE 101: *Nauvoo Temple Wall (restored)*

"LET MY CHILDREN KNOW HOW THE TEMPLE OF NAUVOO WAS BUILT, AND HOW THEIR PARENTS AS WELL AS HUNDREDS OF OTHERS SUFFERED TO LAY A FOUNDATION ON WHICH THEY COULD BUILD AND BE ACCEPTED OF GOD." —*Luman Shurtliff*

the martyrs, their widows, Emma Smith and Mary Fielding Smith, were among the first to see them. "Yea I witnessed their tears, and groans, which was enough to rent the heart of an adamant," wrote Vilate Kimball. "Every brother and sister that witnessed the scene felt deeply to sympathize with them."[38] A few of those present wrote

"The Lord has commanded us to build that temple. We want to build it, but we have not the means. There are people in this city who have the means, but they will not let us have them. What shall we do with such people? I say damn them!" —*Joseph Smith*

"I am very much resigned to my lot, knowing I am justified and have done the best that could be done. Give my love to the children and all my friends;... and as for 'treason'—I know that I have not committed any.... May God bless you all. Amen." — *Joseph Smith*

"O how I loved those men, and rejoiced under their teachings! It seems as if all is gone, and as if my very heart strings will break, and were it not for my beloved wife and dear children I feel as if I have nothing to live for, and would rejoice to be with them in the Courts of Glory." — *Newel Knight*

"Like most of the Lord's anointed in ancient times, [Joseph Smith] has sealed his mission and his works with his own blood; and so has his brother Hyrum. In life they were not divided, and in death they were not separated!" —John Taylor

"When I reflected that our noble chieftain, the Prophet of the living God, had fallen, and that I had seen his brother in the cold embrace of death, it seemed as though there was a void or vacuum in the great field of human existence to me." —*John Taylor*

"I looked upon the Temple and City of Nauvoo as I retired from it and felt to ask the Lord to preserve it as a monument of the sacrifice of his Saints."
— *Wilford Woodruff*

come unto Christ.[5] As two of the promised "millions who shall know brother Joseph again," we express our testimony that he was the "choice seer" whom the Lord raised up to bring forth the word of God. We know that he holds "the keys of this Last Dispensation, and will for ever hold them, both in time and eternity."[6] We are grateful to join with the faithful chorus who sing praises to the man for a life well lived. He was a prophet of God. To this we testify.

"The power that made Nauvoo, that gathered thousands from various climes and kingdoms, that reared the temple, and that whispers to us now, 'Peace be still, and see the salvation of God,' can guide us to bring forth a better city and hundred fold of gathering, and five times as good a temple." — *John Taylor*

15. Pratt, *Autobiography of Parley P. Pratt*, 187.
16. *Western Star* (September 14, 1838), as cited in Stephen C. LeSueur, *The 1838 Mormon War in Missouri* (Columbia: University of Missouri Press, 1987), 48; See Sidney Rigdon Affidavit, July 1, 1843, Smith, *History of the Church*, 3:460.
17. Smith, *History of the Church*, 3:190-91.
18. J. Wickliffe Rigdon, "I Never Knew a Time When I Did Not Know Joseph Smith," 36, as cited in Roger D. Launius, *Alexander William Doniphan: Portrait of a Missouri Moderate* (Columbia, Missouri: University of Missouri Press, 1997), 64.
19. Smith, *History of the Church*, 3:447.
20. Smith, *History of Joseph Smith*, 290-91.
21. Pratt, *Autobiography of Parley P. Pratt*, 192.
22. Smith, *History of the Church*, 3:200-1.
23. Pratt, *Autobiography of Parley P. Pratt*, 193.
24. Pratt, *Autobiography of Parley P. Pratt*, 195.
25. Joseph Smith to Emma Smith, November 12, 1838, as cited in Jessee, *Personal Writings of Joseph Smith*, 368.
26. Pratt, *Autobiography of Parley P. Pratt*, 210-11.
27. E. Robinson, "Items of Personal History," *The Return*, 2 (March 1890): 16, 234, as cited in LeSueur, *The 1838 Mormon War in Missouri*, 198.
27. Joseph Smith to Emma Smith, November 12, 1838, as cited in Jessee, *Personal Writings of Joseph Smith*, 367-68.
28. Smith, *History of the Church*, 3:231-32.
29. Pratt, *Autobiography of Parley P. Pratt*, 212.
30. Smith, *History of the Church*, 3:213.
31. Affidavit of Joseph Smith, et al., March 15, 1839, as cited in Heman C. Smith, ed., "Appeals to Supreme Court of Missouri," *Journal of History* 9 (April 1916) 206.
32. Pratt, *Autobiography of Parley P. Pratt*, 219-20, 222.
33. Jessee, *Personal Writings of Joseph Smith*, 377.
34. Jessee, *Personal Writings of Joseph Smith*, 426.
35. Doctrine and Covenants 121:33.
36. Doctrine and Covenants 121:1-2, 7-10; 122:1, 7-9.
37. Smith, *History of the Church*, 3:423.
38. Pratt, *Autobiography of Parley P. Pratt*, 293.

CHAPTER FOUR

1. Wandle Mace, Autobiography of Wandle Mace, typescript, 102-3.
2. Smith, *History of Church*, 3:375.
3. B. H. Roberts, *A Comprehensive History of the Church of Jesus Christ of Latter-day Saints* (Salt Lake City: Deseret News Press, 1930), 2:9.
4. Smith, *History of the Church*, 3:375.
5. Matthias F. Cowley, *Wilford Woodruff, History of His Life and Labors* (Salt Lake City: Bookcraft, 1975), 104.
6. Smith, *History of Joseph Smith*, 319.
7. Smith, *History of the Church*, 4:133.
8. George A. Smith, "Historical Address by President George A. Smith," *Journal of Discourses*, 13:115.
9. Smith, *History of the Church*, 6:33.
10. Andrus and Andrus, *They Knew the Prophet*, 145.
11. Edwin F. Parry, comp. *Stories about Joseph Smith the Prophet* (Salt Lake City: Deseret News Press, 1934), 22.
12. J. Earl Arrington, "William Weeks, Architect of the Nauvoo Temple," *BYU Studies* 19 (Spring 1979): 341, 346.
13. T. Edgar Lyon, "Recollections of 'Old Nauvooers' Memories from Oral History," *BYU Studies* 18 (Winter 1978): 148.
14. Maureen Ursenbach, "Eliza R. Snow's Journal," *BYU Studies* 15 (Summer 1975): 405-6.
15. Jane Carter Robinson Hindly, "Jane C.Robinson Hindly Reminiscences and Diary," as cited in Richard Neitzel Holzapfel and Jeni Broberg Holzapfel, *Women of Nauvoo* (Salt Lake City: Bookcraft, 1992), 14-15.
16. Doctrine and Covenants 128:22.
17. Wandle Mace Autobiography, 94.
18. B. H. Roberts, *Outlines of Ecclesiastical History*, 3rd ed. (Salt Lake City: Deseret News, 1902), 394.
19. Smith, *History of the Church*, 6:58.
20. Josiah Quincy quoted in E. Cecil McGavin, *Nauvoo, the Beautiful* (Salt Lake City: Bookcraft, 1972), 88-89.
21. *Warsaw Signal* (May 29, 1844).
22. *Warsaw Signal* (June 12, 1844).
23. Horace Cummings, "Conspiracy of Nauvoo," *Contributor* 5 (April 1884): 255.
24. Smith, *History of the Church*, 6:500.
25. Smith, *History of the Church*, 5:259.
26. Smith, *History of the Church*, 6:549, 554.
27. "I Shall Ever Remember My Feelings," *Church News* (June 24, 1984), 11 (translated from the original Welch by Ronald D. Dennis).
28. Roberts, *Comprehensive History*, 2:281.
29. Smith, *History of the Church*, 6:592, 605.
30. James Montgomery, "A Poor Wayfaring Man of Grief," *Hymns of The Church of Jesus Christ of Latter-day Saints* (Salt Lake City: The Church of Jesus Christ of Latter-day Saints, 1985), no. 29, verse 6.
31. Doctrine and Covenants 135:1.
32. Smith, *History of the Church*, 6:618.
33. Doctrine and Covenants 135:1.
34. Doctrine and Covenants 135:7.
35. Smith, *History of the Church*, 7:106.
36. Ronald K. Esplin, "Life in Nauvoo, June 1844: Vilate Kimball's Martyrdom Letters," *BYU Studies* 19 (Winter 1979): 238.
37. William G. Hartley, *"They are My Friends," A History of the Joseph Knight Family, 1825-1850* (Provo, Utah: Grandin Book Company, 1986), 153-54.
38. Esplin, "Life in Nauvoo," 238.
39. Smith, *History of the Church*, 7:156.
40. Roberts, *Comprehensive History*, 2:349-50.

EPILOGUE

1. Bathsheba W. Smith, "Joseph Smith, the Prophet," *Young Woman's Journal* 16 (December 1905): 549-50.
2. *New York Herald*, (July 8, 1844).
3. Smith, *History of the Church*, 7:198.
4. William W. Phelps, "Praise to the Man," *Hymns*, no. 27, verses 1-2.
5. Doctrine and Covenants 109:72-73.
6. Phelps, "Praise to the Man," *Hymns*, No. 27, verse 4; Brigham Young, "Intelligence, etc.," *Journal of Discourses*, 7:289-90.